# DONKEY AND THE FARM TEAM

FOR GRAYSON + RILEY

# ACKNOWLEDGEMENTS

THANKS TO MY WIFE, SARAH

THANKS ALSO TO STEVE STINSON, SUSAN CRITES, ELLEN EMERSON, LYNNE BELL, JEFF PATNAUDE, MOM + DAD, AND MANY OTHERS FOR YOUR TIME, INPUT, GUIDANCE, RECOMMENDATIONS, EXPERIENCES, STORIES, AND MORE. YOU EACH INFLUENCED ME AND ARE DEEPLY APPRECIATED

THE PITCH IS THROWN, THE UMP YELLS "STEEEERIKE!"

LOOK AT THOSE ANIMALS DRESSED IN PINSTRIPES!

ON THE MOUND IS TOAD WITH A BIG LEG KICK.

OUTFIELDERS ARE SHEEP, WHO GRAZE TILL A HIT!

AT SHORT STOP THERE'S GOAT, HIS FIELDING IS FINE.
AT SECOND BASE, CHICKEN, TURNING TWO EVERY TIME!

AT THIRD IS THE HORSE, SHE'S GOT QUITE AN ARM. THROW TO FIRST? WITH EASE, IMPRESSING THE FARM!

THE COW PLAYS FIRST AND BEHIND THE HOME BASE.

DUCK PLAYS CATCHER WITH A MASK ON HIS FACE.

BASEBALL'S LOVED BY ALL ANIMALS ALIKE.

EVEN THE FARMER, THE UMPIRE...STEEEERIKE!

BUT DONKEY'S NO GOOD AND SO HE FEELS SHAME.
HE'S THE ONLY ONE NOT IN LOVE WITH THE GAME.

THE DONKEY GETS TEASED, THEY SAY HE SHOULD QUIT.
HE CAN'T THROW OR CATCH, HE CAN'T EVEN HIT!

ONE DAY HE WAS DOWN, DONKEY LOST A GAME.

HE MOPED OFF THE FIELD, AGAIN FEELING SHAME.

TOAD LOOKED AND NOTICED HOW DONKEY WAS SAD.
HOW OTHERS TEASED DONKEY, IT MADE TOAD MAD.

TOAD HOPPED WITH DONKEY, BACK TO THE STABLE.
"WITH PRACTICE," SAID TOAD, "YOU'LL BE MORE THAN ABLE."

"I'LL HELP YOU LEARN HOW TO THROW, CATCH AND BAT.

WITH TIME YOU'LL GET BETTER, I PROMISE YOU THAT."

"NO SHAME IN LOSING OR HAVING NO SKILL.
YOU NEED ONLY PRACTICE, PATIENCE AND WILL."

"TO GET GOOD TAKES TIME, BUT HOLD YOUR HEAD HIGH.
WIN OR LOSE IT'S A GAME, BUT SURE FUN TO TRY."

"SO LONG AS YOU PRACTICE, GIVE IT YOUR BEST.
SUPPORT YOUR TEAMMATES, AND DON'T SWEAT THE REST."

TOAD HELPED DONKEY, HELPED HIM PRACTICE THE GAME.
DONKEY'S NOT GREAT, BUT HE'S LEARNING, NO SHAME.

IT'S EVENING NOW AND THE CHORES ARE DONE.

THE TEAM RUNS TO THE FIELD TO GO HAVE SOME FUN!

DONKEY'S PLAYED POORLY, BUT HE'S TRIED HIS BEST.
THE GAME'S NEARLY OVER, BUT NOT DONKEY'S TEST.

IT'S THE BOTTOM OF THE NINTH, THE SCORE IS TIED.

DONKEY'S AT BAT, HE'S STRUGGLED BUT TRIED.

TOAD PREPS TO PITCH, HE LOOKS TO THE SKY.

HE WINDS AND DELIVERS, DONKEY HITS HIGH!

DONKEY RUNS TO FIRST, THE BALL STILL FLYING.
HE GOT HIS FIRST HIT BECAUSE HE KEPT TRYING!

AS HE ROUNDS FIRST AND ON TO SECOND BASE,
THE BALL FINALLY LANDS, THE SHEEP GIVE CHASE!

THE SHEEP RUNS AND CATCHES UP TO THE BALL.

IT'S WAY IN RIGHT FIELD THE HIT HIT THE WALL!

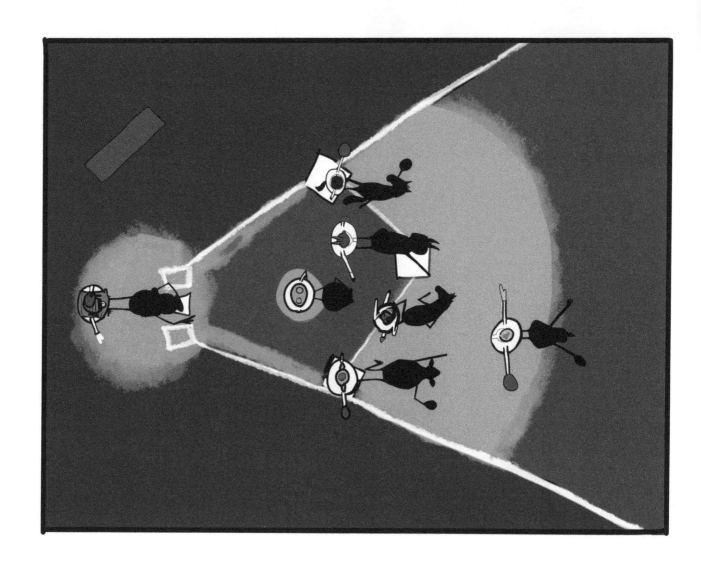

CHICKEN RUNS AND CLUCKS "I'LL CUT OFF THE THROW!"

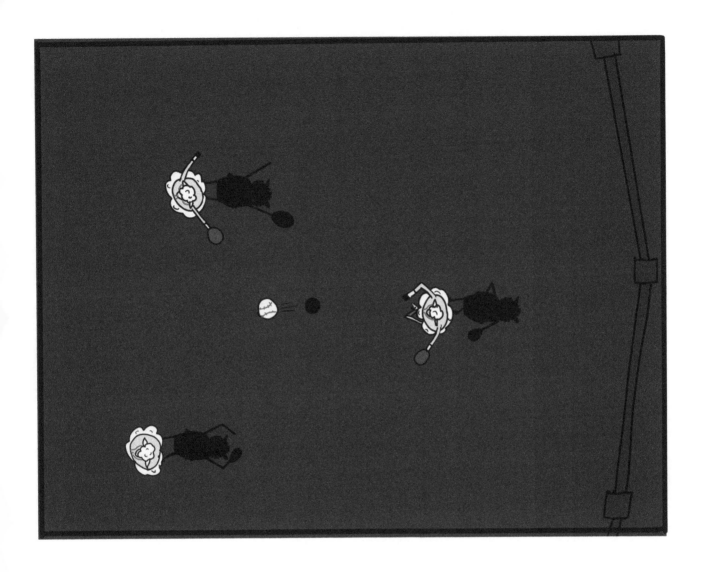

SO SHEEP HURLS TO HIM. OH MY, WHAT A SHOW!

ALL SCORES ARE TIED, ONE OUT LEFT TO PLAY.
IF DONKEY SCORES NOW THEY'LL WIN FOR THE DAY!

ROUNDING 2ND, HIS TEAM CHEERS IN DELIGHT.

THE CUT OFF THROW'S CAUGHT, THIS CALL WILL BE TIGHT!

CHICKEN LOOKS TO THIRD, HE LOOKS WAY TOO LATE.

DONKEY'S HEADED FOR HOME: A SPRINT TO THE PLATE!

IT'S A PERFECT THROW, DUCK'S IN POSITION.

IT'S A RACE: DONKEY OR THROW BY CHICKEN!

THE FARMER LOOKS CLOSELY TO WATCH THE SLIDE.

DONKEY, BALL AND THE DUCK'S GLOVE COLLIDE.

DOWN IS THE TAG, DONKEY SLIDES FOR THE PLATE.

IT'S TOO CLOSE TO TELL IF HE'S OUT OR HE'S SAFE!

THE FARMER JUMPS UP, EXCLAIMS "IT'S A TIE!"
IT'S HAPPENED FAST, IN THE BLINK OF AN EYE!

IN BASEBALL A TIE GOES TO THE RUNNER,
SO DONKEY JUST SCORED, THEY WIN IN A STUNNER!

THEY WIN THE GAME, DONKEY HIT A HOME RUN!

PRACTICE MADE PERFECT, IT MADE THE GAME FUN!

THE FARMER AND TEAM BURST INTO CHEER.

DONKEY'S THE HERO, HE PLAYED WITH NO FEAR!

HAD DONKEY BEEN OUT AND THEY LOST THE GAME.

HE'D HAVE NOT A REASON TO FEEL ANY SHAME.

HOLD YOUR HEAD HIGH, NO MATTER HOW IT ENDS.

GIVE IT YOUR BEST TRY, FOR YOU AND YOUR FRIENDS.

WORK HARD AND PRACTICE EACH TIME YOU PLAY.

YOU'LL BE A HERO LIKE DONKEY ONE DAY!

CPSIA information can be obtained
at www.ICGtesting.com
Printed in the USA
BVHW02*0233131018
529113BV00004B/7/P